Low-Cost Tactics
To
Get More
Blog Traffic

10 Proven Methods to Generate Website
Traffic Without Paying a Cent

Chris Carnell

Disclaimer

This e-book has been written for information purposes only. Every effort has been made to make this ebook as complete and accurate as possible. However, there may be mistakes in typography or content. Also, this e-book provides information only up to the publishing date. Therefore, this ebook should be used as a guide - not as the ultimate source.

The purpose of this ebook is to educate. The author and the publisher does not warrant that the information contained in this e-book is fully complete and shall not be responsible for any errors or omissions. The author and publisher shall have neither liability nor responsibility to any person or entity with respect to any loss or damage caused or alleged to be caused directly or indirectly by this ebook.

About the Author

Chris Carnell is an entrepreneur living in the USA who loves sharing knowledge and helping others on the topic of web technologies.

Chris is a passionate person who will go the extra mile and over-deliver.

Chris's words of wisdom:

"I believe that knowledge is power. Everyone should improve themselves and/or business, no matter what stage in life they're in. Whether it's to develop a better mindset or to increase profits. Moving forward is key."

If you would like to learn more from Chris Carnell, please visit:

http://www.myhowto.online

About the Author

CHAPTER ONE

Introduction

When you have a website, the most important factor in whether or not you are successful – whether your website is trying to sell something or simply trying to get followers and readership – is how much traffic you have.

Traffic is important because it helps you to rank higher in search engines, it helps you to gain expertise in the topic or industry that you're in, it allows you to establish influence and of course, to give you the ability to earn money through affiliate sales, direct sales or even advertising on your website if your traffic is great enough.

But getting traffic these days is tricky. There are millions of competing websites out there and some of them of been around since the dawn of the Internet. In fact, NetCraft announced in late 2014 that there are now over 1 billion websites on the Internet. Without a budget of massive proportions, how do you get traffic to come to your site? SmartInsights says that there are a little less than 3 billion people that are going to be surfing the Internet this year, which is half the world, so how can you get your own little piece of that traffic without having to spend a fortune? In fact, how can you get your own little piece of that traffic without spending a dime? That's exactly what this book is about.

• • • • •

What You'll Learn in This Book

The first thing you'll learn is the number one thing that you have to do before you take a single step towards getting traffic to your website. This thing must be accomplished or else all the traffic in the world won't do any good.

You will learn a killer blogging technique that will allow you to get traffic by blogging a very specific way, and how you can make your readership numbers blow up.

You'll learn how YouTube works and how it can help you to bring traffic to your website by researching how you're going to label your YouTube videos. You'll also learn some YouTube video creation techniques that will help you specifically with getting views on your YouTube videos and then funneling them towards your website.

You'll learn a method for posting a link to your website multiple times a day where could potentially be seen by thousands or even tens of thousands of people, and it won't cost you a single dime.

You'll be able to see example emails that will help you approach people so that you can get traffic to your site from other, more popular websites.

You'll learn how iTunes can help you turn your

trickling website traffic into a huge flowing river of traffic by doing something regularly that is both fun and valuable for people in the same industry as you are.

By the end of this book, you will know how to approach another website or blog and get them to allow you to write a guest post and then put it on their website, in front of all of their visitors, with a link to your website as to drive traffic that way.

You'll learn a method that will allow you to teach a large group of people many of whom will want to visit your website when you're all finished.

You'll learn something new that you may not have known about social media and how you can take advantage of this particular feature so that you can establish yourself as an expert in your industry and be able to gain not only traffic to your website but also a huge amount of social media followers across multiple platforms.

You'll learn what the name dropping method is – a revolutionary new method for getting some of the most influential people on the Internet to link directly to your website without even asking for a link, or anything else for that matter, in return.

You'll also learn how to create a guide or report and make it go viral and then have it drive traffic directly back to your website without you spending a single dime. In fact, other people will distribute this report for you, all leading back to driving traffic to your website for free.

• • • • •

CHAPTER TWO
It All Starts With Your Website

Before you do any traffic generation whatsoever, you first need to make sure that your website is as good as you can possibly make it. This is actually a pretty common mistake.

People spend a great deal of time and money getting traffic to their website without realizing that their conversion rate or bounce rate is all dependent upon how good the website looks. In this chapter, we'll go over some specific tips that will allow you to improve your website and get your numbers where you want them to be.

• • • • •

The Platform

Everything that you'll be doing to improve the look and functionality of your website is based upon the platform that it is running on. WordPress is a very popular platform that offers great functionality, good-looking themes and easy-to-use backend.

Some of the other platforms that people use to build their websites upon include SquareSpace, Wix and Weebly. Of course, how will you are able to improve the look and usability of your website will depend upon your expertise with the platform that you're using or your access to experts that know how to change the design.

That being said, there are lots of ways that even an amateur at WordPress or another website building platform can improve their site using third-party plug-ins and tools. We'll go over some of those in a moment but before you begin you need to ask yourself what you're trying to accomplish in the first place.

What is your goal with your website? Are you trying to convert the casual reader into a paying customer? Are you trying to entice someone to come back and read your blog posts again and again? Whatever your goal is, you need to decide upon it and keep it in mind while you are improving the look of your site.

If your goal is to get your readers to become customers – which means they actually spend money at your site – you are going to need a really great looking site with all of the right trust symbols and the most professional design possible. However, even if you are just trying to attract a new follower the more professional that your site looks more willing they will be to come back.

• • • • •

Tools You Can Use to Improve the Look of Your Site

One of the most popular tools out there made specifically for WordPress is a plugin called

OptimizePress. This is a plugin with all kinds of features and templates that you can use to build landing pages, sales pages or whatever your website needs, and make them look amazing.

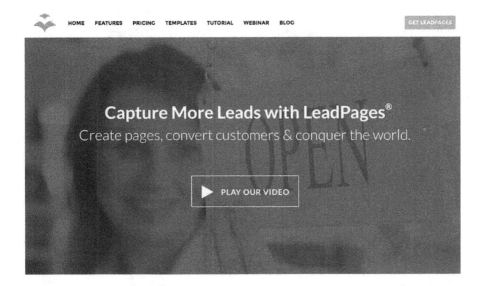

LeadPages.net is also a great resource for sales page templates and much more.

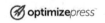

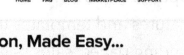

Marketing Site Creation, Made Easy...

OptimizePress is the new way to create high converting landing pages, sales pages and membership portals

- Create Sales Pages
- Converting Landing Pages
- Membership Portals
- Complete Launch Funnels
- Authority Blog Sites

Click Here To Get OptimizePress
Start building your site in under 15 minutes

00:00   HD

While this book is about ways of getting traffic to your website without spending any money, one of the things that you should spend money on is your website design; make sure that your site looks as professional as possible, even if you have to spend a little money to get there.

The tools that you will use depend entirely upon what platform your website is based upon and there are literally thousands out there. If you're looking to use tools or third-party applications to design your landing pages, squeeze pages or sales pages here are a few things to keep in mind.

You get what you pay for – to a certain point. There is no standard pricing for applications or plugins so you have to shop around and find which one is going to do the best job for you with the best deal.

Don't fall into the trap of paying a monthly subscription price. Find something that will work for you that you can pay for and then own, to create as many sales pages or landing pages as you want in the future.

Make sure that you can test the product before you buy it. There should be some sort of trial that you can download or some other method for you to test the software without actually having to pay for. Don't rely on flashy video because it may not work the same for you and you may find it is not what you're looking for after all.

Make sure that a guarantee comes with your product. If it doesn't work as advertised or simply doesn't work for you, you want to be able to return it and get your money back. Many of these programs offer a money back guarantee. You just have to look for them.

• • • • •

Signs of a Professional Website

Here are some of the signs and features that show people a site is professional and trustworthy. Make sure that your website has as many of these factors as you can.

The colors of the website are carefully chosen and complementary. Amateur websites will have contrasting, mismatched colors.

The images are of the highest quality and are completely relevant to the content that they surround.

All of the website copy is professionally written, geared towards a specific purpose and is completely free of typos and grammar mistakes.

The design of your website or your template is updated and stylish for the current year. There are many WordPress templates out there that are several years old and haven't been updated.

Your website, Twitter, Facebook and all of the other online properties that you have, match when it comes to the theme and design. You want to be using the same colors, the same logos and the same fonts across all of your properties.

It should go without saying that your website needs to display properly on all of the mobile devices that are out there. You will have no problem finding WordPress themes that are responsive but make sure that you test your website out before starting your traffic generation techniques because not every responsive theme works well with every type of site.

With all that noted, you're now ready to start generating traffic to your website!

The first method that we're going to discuss to get traffic to your website without spending a dime is the viral blogging method.

What exactly is viral blogging? Viral blogging is when you purposely post content that is most likely to be shared and therefore, go viral. You might think that every piece of content that you post is specifically intended to be shared and go viral possible, but the difference is that you choose your topics and the format of your posts in very specific ways, that have been shown to be most effective for viral content.

We are going to go over some of these specific content types and show you how to give your posts the best chance to go viral.

How To Get Started With This Method

There are some things that you're going to want to do no matter what type of content you are posting. These are tips that are the same for all of the content that you're planning on posting. The first tip is to post on a regular basis. People are more likely to come back and read your content over and over again if you post regularly.

This means posting once a week, preferably on the same day, or whatever your schedule happens to be. You can post every five days, you could post once every two weeks or however you'd like. What you should keep in mind is that you need post regularly enough so that people don't forget about your content, which generally means posting at least once per week, but not so often that people are overwhelmed by it and can't read it all. You always want to leave them wanting more.

Keep in mind that you don't have to write and post your content when you're scheduled to publish it. If you're using WordPress, you can schedule your content to be published on a specific date and time and you can write several weeks in advance if you prefer.

Another thing that you want to do is make sure that you use your keywords in both the title and in the post. Do you know what your keywords are supposed to be? If not, you need to do some keyword research and find out what keyword phrases are being searched for when it comes to the content that you're planning on publishing. Try to find a happy medium between keyword phrases the get a lot of searches and those phrases that have a ton of competition already on the first page of Google results.

As mentioned in the beginning of this book, high-quality images are vital. Make sure that you include images with your content and that they are both high-quality and relevant to the text on the page.

Also, make sure that you don't pack everything into huge, intimidating blocks of text. Create subheadings so that people can skim the content, and break your text into several different paragraphs with a general rule of no more than 100 words per paragraph. You can have less, and you can even have a little bit more, but use it as a general rule of thumb and remember, varying paragraph lengths are more interesting than several paragraphs in a row all of the same length.

Viral Blogging Content Types

Now, were going to discuss some of the different types of content that are great for creating viral posts that are more likely to be shared than anything else. Each of these types of content is unique and has a different style than other types on this list. With some types of content you may want to include humor or lighthearted writing, and with others you want to avoid humor and take a more serious approach.

In case you're wondering where this information comes from there have been several studies of different content types to determine what gets shared most often. The market research company BuzzSumo recently analyzed over 100 million articles to discover what gets shared and the results include the post types listed below.

Top Ten Lists

For some reason, top 10 lists seem to do particularly well on social media. In fact, it is specifically the number 10 in top 10 lists the does well.

10 New Uses for Zucchini
sparkpeople.com - More from this domain
By Sparkpeople guest Blogger - Apr 29, 2015
Article

% View Backlinks
👥 View Sharers **3.0k**
⪦ Share

10 Slimming Smoothie Recipes
prevention.com - More from this domain
By Prevention Magazine - Dec 1, 2015
Article

% View Backlinks
👥 View Sharers **1.8k**
⪦ Share

10 Colored Nails You Must Try This Season - Beautythere
beautythere.com - More from this domain
By Beautythere - Jun 13, 2015
Article

% View Backlinks
👥 View Sharers **29**
⪦ Share

No one knows exactly why this is; it might be because ten is a nice round number or could be because 8 items are too few to make up a decent list and 15 are too many; whatever the reason, research shows the top 10 lists should be part of your viral blogging strategy.

News and Current Events Articles

Not surprisingly, posting the latest news or current events will not only get you noticed, it will also get your content shared. When someone learns something that is considered news their first instinct is to share with others. Of course, if you learn about things after they have already been posted to most of the major news organizations and websites, creating an article on that news story won't do you much good. If you can "scoop" other news organizations and get your posts in front of people, the chances are very good that they will share it.

Controversial Topics and Titles

Another content type that is sure to get shared with others (and as a bonus get all kinds of comments posted underneath it) is the controversial topic – with a controversial title. This is especially potent if you can combine controversy with the current event, with the disadvantage of the content not lasting very long. You can also create controversy with blog posts and titles that are evergreen which will keep getting traffic for years to come.

Entertainment and Celebrity News

One content type that is certainly popular is celebrity and entertainment news. The problem is, there is a lot of competition for these articles and topics. There are websites that dominate this market because they cover celebrity entertainment news exclusively. However, that doesn't mean you should ignore this content type altogether.

Should These Celebrities Delete Their Twitter Accounts? Some Unsolicited Advice

13h ago

Amber Rose Is Unrecognizable In This Cheesy Middle School Pic

13h ago

Justin Bieber's New Puppy Is The Cutest Thing You'll See All Day

18h ago

hip-hop

Drake Will Put His True Ping Pong Greatness To The Test Against A Hall Of Famer

19h ago

You can cover a celebrity and tie it in with your industry. As a hypothetical example, if you were in the business industry, you could talk about how Drake invested in a new company.

Politics

Of course, politics is always one of the hot button topics on the Internet. This is a case where publishing a political and controversial article may get your content shared with millions of others. You can always mix two of these types and get better results but politics, combined with controversy in particular, seem to be a potent combination for sharing.

The great thing about this particular topic is that you can share an opinion if you like without any real factual basis – unless of course you are quoting facts to back up your opinions.

How to Promote Your Content

Simply publishing this content isn't going to be enough. You need to promote your content on social media – but not just the standards like Facebook, Twitter and Pinterest.

You also want to use social bookmarking sites like Digg, Reddit and StumbleUpon. These sites will get you in front of readers who will hopefully take your content and run with it.

Another method that you can use to get traffic to your website is to make videos for the popular sharing website YouTube. YouTube sees around 1 billion users every single month and so posting a video on YouTube almost guarantees that it will be seen as long as you use the right keywords.

In this article, we'll explore the process of making a video – and making it professional enough to attract traffic to your site – as well as the process of choosing keywords and getting it published on YouTube.

Step One: Making the Video

The first thing you're going to have to do is make the video. What kind of video should you make? You can make whatever kind of video you want but keep in mind that your goal is to get people to watch the entire thing and want to know more afterwards. You want them to read the description and look for a link and then leave the YouTube site to come to your own website.

So, this could be a how-to video. These types of videos are quite popular on YouTube and they are ready made to send traffic to your website because if you give them almost all of the information that they need with the video and then promise them the rest if they go to your website, this will drive traffic.

You don't want to make a video to simply promote your business because people aren't going to want to watch it in the first place, nor are they going to want to come to your website afterward. But if you can make a funny or awesome video that evokes emotion, and features your business as part of it, then you'll be able to get YouTube views and traffic to your website as well as shares.

If you're going to stick to the methods of getting traffic without any money spent, you're going to have to create the video yourself. However, there are websites out there like Fiverr that will allow you to outsource video production very inexpensively. If you have to go DIY, making a video isn't too difficult to do on your own anyway and you might find that you have a talent at it.

Step Two: Getting Your Keywords

The next step we are going to take will be getting the keywords that you will use in the title and tag sections of your YouTube video.

Your first task is to determine whether anyone is actually searching for the keywords that you've chosen. Obviously, with keywords like 'money' or 'investing' you don't have to look and see if anyone is searching; you know that millions of people are using the search terms. But there is no way that you can compete for these search terms on YouTube without many years of hard work so what you're looking for our search terms that only get a few searches (but still get some) and that are much easier to compete for on YouTube.

You want to use the Adwords Keyword Planner (https://adwords.google.com/KeywordPlanner)

because it is the number one tool for finding out what kind of usage a search term actually gets. You can just type in your search terms and see the estimated monthly traffic that a search term gets to make your decision based upon that. Now, that isn't going to be the search traffic that that term gets on YouTube, but it will give you an idea as to what is popular when it comes to searching and what is not.

Go For Low-Hanging Fruit

One trick is to go for "low-hanging fruit". This means intentionally going for keywords for your videos to get a very specific group of people to take action. Typically the keywords are longer tail.

The advantage of going for low-hanging fruit is that you'll capture a more targeted audience and get ranked on YouTube easier. If you were to go for a broader term such as "weight loss", it would be near impossible to rank these days.

You won't get as many people searching for longer tail keywords, but at least you'll gain higher quality viewers.

This is where you can "rinse and repeat" this

method.

Step Three: Publishing the Video

Finally, your last step would be publishing the video. There are many different ways that you can do this and one of the easiest is to publish it directly from your video editing program.

Of course, instead you could just publish it directly on YouTube. You'll need to have exported it from your video editing program or uploaded it from your camera if you didn't do any editing, and it will need to fit certain specifications like having the right file format, following YouTube's size guidelines and other considerations.

You can find out exactly what YouTube requires when you upload a video by going to your YouTube page and clicking 'Upload'. Once you have your video uploaded, you can create the title and set your tags. Then, you can go ahead and publish it. It will be on YouTube and driving traffic to your website shortly.

The next method of getting traffic to your site without spending any money that we're going to discuss is forum marketing. There are millions of forums out there dedicated to every topic imaginable. You are certain to find active and growing forums built around your particular topic. In fact, you may already be a member of some of these forums and up until now have just participated in the discussions, asked and answered questions or simply kept up with what other people are saying about your industry.

Your Signature Is Your Salesman

Forums can be one of the most effective marketing methods that you can use. However, you have to find the right forum that allows you to create a link to your website that people can easily click on. This is done through your forum signature. Your signature may be composed of text, images, HTML and links that lead directly back to your website.

If you are joining a new forum, or thinking about posting somewhere that you haven't been active before, the first thing that you need to do is determine whether or not you can put a link in your signature that will be visible and attractive enough for people to click on, so that you can get traffic to your website from that forum. If the forum does not allow links in your signature or renders them so small as to not be useful, avoid posting on that forum and go somewhere else.

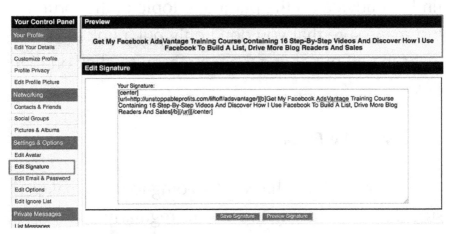

This is where you put your signature on the Warrior Forum

What to put on your signature is going to take some thought. What you need to understand, is that your signature is intended to provide people with an easy-to-follow link to your website without being obtrusive. So, you don't want a forum signature where you have a giant link to your site in bright red that looks ugly and completely overpowers anything else on the forum. You do want a visible and easy-to-follow link. More importantly than that, you want to give people a reason to follow the link.

That means, you need to create some sort of reason using the text or images in your signature. For example, you can invite them to get something for free or take advantage of a special offer or even to find out advice on the particular topic of the forum. Just make sure that you don't only put a link to your website without giving them a reason to click on that link.

Using the Forums

The next thing that you're going to do is make sure that you're using the forums regularly. Remember, each time you post on the forums you are basically posting another advertisement for your website. You never know who is going to see it, so spend as much time as you're able – without giving the impression that you are spamming the forum – on answering questions, giving advice and providing useful and valuable content.

Another thing that you should keep in mind when it comes to forums is that you might want to expand your horizons a little bit. Many forum users tend to stick to just one or two sections where they most enjoy posting. That means, if you stay in those one or two sections, you are going to be advertising your link to pretty much the same people. But if you go out and post in other parts of the forum you are likely going to be showing your signature to a huge, new group of people.

Responding to the posts made on a thread you created is important as well. Some people are going to arrive at the thread and only read the last few posts. That means that your particular post may be a long way back and they aren't even going to see it but if you reply to other posts – and remember you need to say something valuable not just reply to be replying – then whoever visits the forum will always be able to see your signature in one of your replies.

You may not always be able to create a signature with a link in it. However, you still should be able to include some sort of information in your signature and even if you can't – like if the forum doesn't offer a signature – you'll probably be able to include website links in your bio. However, relying on your bio to send traffic to your website is rather iffy, and you have to make doubly sure that you write informative, valuable posts that people will make people want to find out who the author is and check them out elsewhere on the web. Is a much better idea to find a forum that offers a signature, but if you do have a particular forum that is very active or is laser targeted at your audience, you might still want to participate once in a while to have access to those users.

Other Signature Ideas

Another thing that you should be aware of is that forums aren't the only places where you can include a signature. You can almost always include a signature on your email, which means that everyone that you send an email to will get a link to your website. This is an unobtrusive way to advertise to your email contacts. There may be other places online where you regularly post or participate that allows you to have a bio or signature as well, that you're not currently taking advantage of.

Tactic #3: The Forum Authority Method

Our next method is called the thank you page method and it is a way for you to get traffic to your site directly from another site that is related to yours, or in some cases, even a competitor of yours. You might be wondering why a competitor of yours – or even a related site – would be willing to put a link to your website on theirs.

That's exactly why this method works. You need to give them a reason to link back to your website. There are also a few other things that you have to keep in mind in order to use this method effectively and you may have to skip this technique altogether if your site is brand-new.

The Professionalism of Your Website

The first thing to be aware of is that the professionalism of your website is going to determine (at least partially) whether or not you are able to use this technique. You need to make your website look as good as possible, as mentioned in the very first chapter, in order to make this work, because you are going to be trading links with other websites and they aren't going to want to have their link posted on a website that doesn't look professional.

Also, they're not going to want their link posted on the website that doesn't have anything to offer them. For example, if your website is brand-new, Google isn't going to care too much about links from you to their website. That's especially true if you are linking to each other. Most of the time, links cancel each other out anyway. But this is only a concern if the person linking to your website is doing it to get a link back to raise their rankings in the search engines.

However, if you are simply linking to each other so that you can send traffic to your respective websites, this is something that is valuable enough for most people to want to trade with you. But your website still has to be professional. If you put a link to their website on your thank you page, people will go to their website only when they have already finished their purchase or email opt in from you and conversely, you will only get traffic from the other website when visitors that site reach the thank you page.

How to Use This Technique

Your first task if you're going to use this technique is finding some similar websites that have thank you pages that you might be able to approach. Don't be afraid to approach a website as long as you have made your own site as professional looking as possible. Other Internet marketers and website owners are always looking for ways to generate more traffic and if your method brings even a few more people to their website and doesn't cost them anything or reduce their existing website traffic and anyway, they are sure to be on board with it.

Search the site until you find their contact email and then write them a message asking them if they would be interested in the thank you page link exchange. You can compare this to the way that Amazon shows people related content after they purchase something. The customer will have already purchased an item from your partner and so he or she will have nothing to lose by sending traffic your way.

Be polite and be persistent. If someone doesn't respond to you, it probably means that they were not interested in pursuing your offer. You might get a dozen rejections and this is frustrating, but don't give up because the 13th could be the one that says yes and then drives a ton of traffic to your site. It is a win-win situation for both of you and it cost nothing but a few seconds to put a link on your page. Cross-promotion is one of the most effective Internet marketing methods. Below is an example email that you can send.

Name,

I noticed that you had a great product for sale on your website. {NameofProgram} seems as if it would be a very valuable resource for my customers as well as yours, as I sell a very similar product. I wondered if you would be interested in doing a 'Thank You' page link exchange where I would place a banner on my thank you page that would link to your product in return for you doing the same for mine. If you want to check out my site and the product that I am offering this is the link: http://www.nameofyoursite.com. Please let me know if you would like to proceed and provide me with a banner or link so that we can get the process started.

    Sincerely,

    Your Name

The podcasting method is a great way to get the word out there about you and your product or service. Podcasts are sort of like radio broadcasts except that they are stored on the Internet and can be played whenever the listener chooses. This is a great way to get traffic to your website because you're able to offer your podcast free-of-charge on websites like the Apple iTunes Store where you could potentially get thousands of downloads per podcast.

RealTalk!
RealTalk! Business is ...

Marketing With Vino
Quintin Venter & Gaby...

Confessions of a
Female Entrepreneur
Alyssa Martin :: Entre...

The Robin Sharma
Mastery Sessions
Robin Sharma

Investing In The U.S. -
An Aussie's Guide t...
Reed Goossens

Jocko Podcast
Jocko Podcast

Chase Your
Impossible with...
Inspired by Brendon .

TheEdTalks | Helping
Busy People Feel...
Ed Donato | A Health ...

The Authority Hacker
Podcast: Learn Onli...
Gael Breton - Blogger...

YWoman Show,
Inspiring Interviews...
Shar Moore, YWoman...

Podcasts ▾
Business ▾

PODCAST QUICK LINKS
Redeem   Account
Send iTunes Gifts   Support

Podcast Resources
Submit a Podcast

New Releases
Featured Providers
Language Learning
Making a Podcast

TOP EPISODES >
1.   #681: The Oil
   Planet Money   Kingdom

Why People Listen to Podcasts

There are many different reasons that people listen to podcasts. Some people just enjoy talk radio but they are on the Internet so they can have talk radio that is geared towards their specific field of interest. Some people listen to podcasts while they're in their car driving. Some people enjoy listening to podcasts while they're doing something else on the Internet such as a graphic designer working in Photoshop at the same time that he or she is listening.

People love the portability of podcasts. They can load them onto their smartphone or iPod and then take that podcast with them wherever they go. People also love the convenience of being able to stop or pause and then come back to that podcast later on. But most of all, people want to hear about things that interest them. If you are a comic book collector, you'd love to listen to a podcast on comic book collecting. If you are a woodworking enthusiast, a woodworking podcast would be your cup of tea.

How to Create a Podcast

If you're going to create a podcast, there are a few things that you need in order to get traffic. That's because only a high-quality podcast that is valuable and entertaining to the listeners is going to drive traffic to your website. If your podcast is unprofessional or boring they may listen for a few minutes but they will soon move on to something else and never visit your website.

So, the first thing that you're going to need to create a podcast is some sort of entertaining content. This will mean that you need to research what you're going to talk about and find something that can provide value to your listeners and then figure out a way to present it so that it is also entertaining. If you sit in front of your microphone and simply discuss the topic in a monotone, without any entertainment value at all, people are not going to listen to your podcasts.

Speaking of microphones, you need to have a great one for podcasting. Luckily, there are some out there that are extremely high quality for a very low price.

The Audio-Technica brand makes good microphones for around $50-$75. Also, the Blue Yeti is almost a studio quality microphone for about $100.

You'll need to do your research and decide on your particular professional microphone, but make sure that it is clear without any fuzziness or distortion.

You also need to figure out where you're going to record your podcast. You want to record it somewhere where there is almost no noise. If you have a fan going – like your computer fan – or you have other noises such as kids running around, dogs barking or traffic this is going to make for a very low quality podcast. You need to make sure that you can do your podcast somewhere away from all the noise so that it sounds as professional as a radio broadcast.

You might think about getting a partner as well. This can actually be done over the Internet. Find someone who has the same microphone that you do and then each of you record your part of the podcast separately on the same recording software – Audacity is a good, free solution – while communicating with each other via Skype or another program that allows you to talk to each other instantly.

Then, one of you can receive the audio file from the other one line it up with the audio file that they have and then exported as one new audio file which will have both of your voices recorded with good microphones and it will seem like both of you were in the same studio recording at the same time.

You also might want to think about some theme music or what is known in the radio business as a liner or station ID, which you can often get free of charge on a site called RadioDaddy. If not you can always spend five bucks and get one from Fiverr, but that could come later if you like. This will give your podcast that polished feel that will make people want to listen again and again.

Hosting Your Podcast For Free

Once you've made your recordings, where do you store the audio files?

You can use paid services such as Libsyn which starts at $5.00 per month, but that is the paid route and would defeat the purpose of the zero-cost method.

Instead, you can use free storage services such as Google Drive to store your recordings. What you'll be doing is create a new folder in your Google Drive dedicated to your podcast audio files.

This article by Digital Inspiration will guide you step-by-step: http://www.labnol.org/internet/host-podcasts-on-google-drive/28227/

Distributing Your Podcast

The last thing that you're going to worry about is distributing your podcast. You're going to need to post it somewhere where people can download or listen to it online or via their mobile device.

The best place to distribute your podcast is through the iTunes store. With millions of people on, you can grab your share of the podcasting audience.

The iTunes store is a very good source for listeners but it isn't the only place out there. You can find all kinds of places online where you can post your podcast free-of-charge that will get traffic to your site because you have people listening to it.

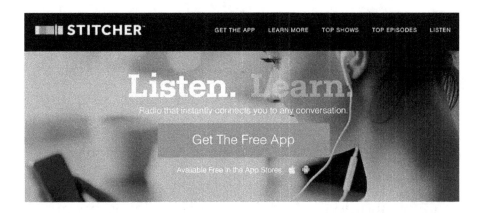

The more places that you posted, the more traffic you will get. Some of these places include: Stitcher (http://stitcher.com), SoundCloud (http://soundcloud.com) and many more podcasting directories that may allow you to submit your podcast for free.

In this chapter, were going to discuss how you can guest post for other blogs and websites in order to drive traffic to your website. Now, you might think that you have to be a pretty decent writer in order to use this method and unless you are willing to spend money on outsourcing or have a friend that is a good writer is willing to do you a favor, you are right. However, if you are a terrible writer, it doesn't mean that you should discard the idea completely because it can be one of the most valuable ways that you can get traffic.

Why Guest Posting Works

So, why would someone allow you to post on their website or blog anyway? The simple answer is, because it provides value to the readers and it something that they didn't have to write themselves or outsource themselves. However, the key word here is providing value to the readers. If your post does not teach the reader something or entertain them it could actually work against their blog instead of for it. So, if you're going to use this method you definitely have to make sure that whatever you're providing is valuable content.

The thing is, if you provide this valuable content to the people that are reading the blog, they are going to want to know more about the author of the content that they enjoyed. That means that if you have a visible link to your website at the end of the article or blog post, or if you have a biography page or snippet right there on the blog post itself, people are going to follow it and come to your website. This is great for you because all it cost you to get this traffic was a couple hours writing a good blog post.

How to Write a Guest Post

Writing a guest post for someone else's blog can be a little different than writing for your own. For example, author Chuck Wendig uses a great deal of profanity on his blog, but if he did a guest post for the American Library Association blog, it is very likely that he would eliminate his use of profanity for that particular post; at least, hopefully. For some blogs, you can write in your own style and that is okay with them. In fact, it is the way that some people prefer to have guest posters write.

Others would rather that you looked at their blog posts and followed the same sort of general writing guidelines as the other people that have guest posted or their own blog posts. When you communicate with someone about guest posting on their blog, you'll need to ask them which method they prefer and for any writers guidelines that they want you to follow.

Make sure that you're actually approaching blogs that are involved within your industry because approaching a random blog on fashion when your particular niche is dog grooming is not only going to get your email blocked, it wouldn't do you any good anyway, even if they were willing to let you guest post. You want to communicate with the same type of audience that would want to come to your website in the first place and that means posting on blogs that are similar to the products or services that you sell.

Also, keep in mind that you have this one chance to sell yourself to the readers of this blog. That means, you need to make this post as high-quality as you possibly can. Make sure that you set it aside for a few days and then come back to revise it so that you can see any mistakes. Better yet, have a friend or relative that is a regular reader look it over for you and point out any mistakes.

You also need to look out for any typos or grammar mistakes is this will make you look amateurish and the one will follow the link to your website. Make it the best post that you possibly can, and make it is useful and valuable to the readers as you can, and you might get invited back to guest post over and over again, each time with a link to your website.

How to Approach Someone to Request a Guest Posting Spot

You might be wondering, what exactly you should do or say to get someone to allow you to post on their blog as a guest. Obviously, you first need to send them an email and see if they allow guest posting for one thing, and at the same time, sell yourself and your expertise so that they want to use you. Below is an example email that you can use to ask someone to give you a guest posting Spot on their blog.

Name,

I really love your blog. I especially enjoyed your post on (name a post you particularly liked) and I agree with you wholeheartedly. I am also an industry expert with a website. I love to write a blog post for you sometime if you would consider linking back to my site from that post. I can either create it from scratch or you can give me a topic that you have been thinking about covering and I will write it. I can assure you that it will be very high quality content from an expert in the industry. Let me know if you're interested.

Sincerely,

Your Name

you@yoursite.com

Have you ever thought about holding a webinar session? Whatever industry you are in, it is likely that you know enough about the industry to actually teach other people something about it. A webinar is a great way to share this information with people and usually you won't have a problem attracting people to your webinar because it's live and people know that they can ask questions and that they will almost certainly learn something of value. In fact some people make a living just holding webinars on the Internet, on whatever industry or topic they are an expert in.

What to Hold a Webinar on

So, you need to decide on something that you

can hold a webinar on. First of all, you want to pick something specific. Let's use the example of graphic design. You can't hold a webinar on how to teach people to do graphic design because the topic is so comprehensive that it would take you hundreds if not thousands of webinars to cover everything that is involved in becoming a graphic designer. There are hundreds and hundreds of books published on just Photoshop alone each year.

But what you can do is pick something specific that you can teach people. For example, suppose you are teaching beginning graphic design students how to remove the redeye effect from old photographs? This might be a valuable lesson for them and something that they are willing to spend an hour learning how to do. So the first step is to choose something specific that you can share with people that is related to your industry or website.

You also need to make a plan for what you are going to teach them, unless it is a question-and-answer webinar, because if you go into a webinar unprepared and you fly by the seat of your pants you probably aren't going to give them the best experience. Of course, that all depends on your teaching style, but remember, your goal is to get them to look you up afterward because what you taught them was valuable and memorable.

Finally, while some people – in fact many people – charge for webinars, you're going to offer yours for free. Remember, the goal is to drive traffic to your website and that means getting as many people as possible to come to the webinar in the first place. You can advertise your free webinar on many of the same places that are outlined in this book – like forums for example.

How to Hold a Webinar

So, how do you hold a webinar anyway? There are several different ways that you can hold a webinar. You could go the very simple route of using Google Hangouts but the problem with this method is that you have a very limited ability to communicate by images, drawings or animations. You simply have your web cam and your microphone in order to communicate with the people attending your Google hangout.

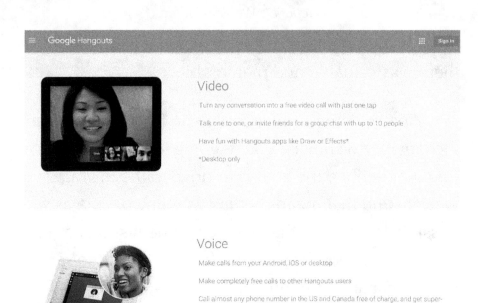

Video

Turn any conversation into a free video call with just one tap

Talk one to one, or invite friends for a group chat with up to 10 people

Have fun with Hangouts apps like Draw or Effects*

*Desktop only

Voice

Make calls from your Android, iOS or desktop

Make completely free calls to other Hangouts users

Call almost any phone number in the US and Canada free of charge, and get super-low rates on international calls*

There are also applications that are specifically intended for things like over-the-Internet conferences and webinars that basically allow you to have access to a whiteboard that everyone at your webinar can see. You can write on the whiteboard, post images and even play videos. These applications are intended for you to be able to communicate with your audience through a variety of ways. The better ones do cost money but you can find some free ones out there if you look.

There are free webinar platforms available on the web, one option is Meeting Burner (https://www.meetingburner.com/). There's a free option to hold a webinar with up to 10 attendees.

How to Promote Your Free Webinar

If you want to get people to attend your webinar, you're going to have to get the word out somehow. This seems challenging, because it seems like if you knew how to get the word out about your webinar you could just get the word out about your website. The difference is, it is a lot easier to get people to help you promote a free webinar on something that they're interested in or something that they work in, than it is to get people to send traffic to your website for your own profit or gain.

Of course, the first thing that you'll need to do is promoted on social media. You may already have a following on social media sites and if that is the case this might be a source of attendees for your webinar. Even if you don't have very many followers, the ones that you do have may promote your webinar if they see it on Twitter or Facebook. This is especially true if they know that you have something valuable to offer.

The way that you word your advertisement or announcement will have a big impact on how many people sign up. If you can let people know that they're going to get something valuable by attending, and that you are an expert in the field that they should listen to, you are definitely going to get twice as many people signing up, and don't forget to promote the fact that it's free.

Finally, approach people in your industry that are on the web and let them know about your free webinar and ask them if they might consider promoting it. Since it's free, they might think it is valuable enough that their own followers would want and they may promote it for you. You can find people within your industry by looking at some of the top websites in your particular niche and then contacting the information or support emails.

You can also look on forums and places where your active that involve your industry and ask some of the top people there if they would promote your free webinar. Don't forget, you can also promote yourself on these forums where you are active.

Tactic #8: The Social Media Groups Traffic

SOCIAL MEDIA GROUPS TRAFFIC

In chapter nine, we're going to discuss how you can use social networking groups to drive content to your website. You know what social media is, but did you know there are actually many social networking groups out there for almost every social media platform and covering almost every topic imaginable. People build communities around even the most eclectic of interests, and so if you look long enough you will find something in your industry on every social media website that you have an account at.

However, don't let the lack of one stop you. Even if you don't have an account or don't usually use the social networking site, and you find that there is a group there that fits your topic, go ahead and sign up for that social media platform and start using it. These groups are invaluable when it comes to driving traffic to your website because not only will people come and visit your website from encountering you within the group, they will also send people over to your website if they consider you an expert and content on your website or products that you sell solve the problem for them.

Starting Your Own Group

If there isn't a group in your social media circles for the industry that you are in, don't be afraid to start one. In fact, since your goal is to be looked at as an expert in this industry so that people want to come to your website, starting a Facebook group or group on some other social media platform, could be one of the best things that you can do.

You may find that once you create the group and post about it to people who might be interested in it that you'll soon have a sizable following and quite a bit of traffic coming to your site.

Benefits of Joining and Participating in Social Media Groups

There are a lot of benefits to being part of a social media group that is built around your topic or industry. For one thing, you have the visibility that comes with being a member and having your website information on your bio or anyplace within group posts where they allow you to place a link to your website.

If you can answer questions about the industry

and give people good advice you will quickly build up a reputation as an expert in the field. This will make even more people want to ask you questions and get advice from you and it will entice people to check you out outside of the group setting, which means they will be going to your website.

But building a reputation as an expert in that industry doesn't just apply to the Facebook group or whatever social media group you are part of. Once people know your name and know you as an expert you are able to write articles and posts on other websites forums where people might already be aware of your expertise. This means that you will have an easier time getting a foot in the door at other endeavors that you are working on as an expert in that industry.

For example, it will be easier to do many of the things that are discussed in this book. When it comes to guest posting, you will have a definite advantage from your participation in social media groups within your industry. That's because not only can you use your membership to convince people to allow you to guest post on their blog, you'll probably be able to find people within your own group that will allow you to guest post in return for a link. In fact, they will be happy to have your expertise on their blog if they consider you a leader or a knowledgeable person within the social media group that you're in.

Social Media Groups Give You Clout and Followers

When you are part of a social media group around a particular industry, and you begin to build a reputation as an expert, people start to listen to your opinions. This means that you can make product recommendations and give advice that may result in you being able to earn affiliate commissions or other monetary rewards. However, this is a great responsibility and so you want to be careful to only promote things that you are sure are valuable to those you are influencing. You will lose all of your credibility if you begin to promote items that are worthless just to make money from your followers.

Speaking of followers, you'll be able to increase your following by joining these groups by a huge amount. For example, if you're part of a Facebook group people are going to want to follow you on your Facebook account if they like what your posting. No matter what your social media platform, if it has a group you have a chance of gaining followers and not just on that social networking site but also on the major social networking sites where they can find you. If they stumble on your account on Twitter they'll follow you because they know you from the Facebook group.

There is no doubt that Facebook and other social media groups have enormous benefits for someone who is looking to market their website without spending any money. These groups are free to join and only require an investment of your time and expertise to pay dividends.

Some other social media platforms with groups functionality you want to get involved in are:

LinkedIn Groups - https://www.linkedin.com/directory/groups/

Google+ Communities - https://plus.google.com/communities

Future Technology
285,544 members   19,729 posts
Join

Accelerating Technolog...
25,421 members   2,467 posts
Join

TECHnology NEWS
216,025 members   26,305 posts
Join

Amazing Technology
5,387 members   459 posts
Join

Genius in Wearable Tec...
2,344 members   1,692 posts
Join

Computer & Information...
10,394 members   1,040 posts
Join

Electrical Technology
1,725 members   1,424 posts
Ask to join

Wearable Technology - ...
5,446 members   367 posts
Join

In this chapter, were going to discuss a unique method of getting traffic to your site without spending a dime called the name dropping method. This is a very easy and very effective way to get traffic to your website. The first thing that you need to understand is that some people on the Internet have more influence than others. People that are influencers tend to have fans that will follow their recommendations almost unwaveringly.

That means, if they post a link to your website on their website or on their social media platforms, their followers are going to want to see what it is. Those followers are going to click on the link simply because they respect the person that gave it to them. You could get a huge amount of traffic if one of these influencers decides to post to your website or mention your name somehow. This method is a terrific way to get that done.

How It Works

So, your first step is going to be writing an article. Again, if you're not a writer you're either going to have to find a friend that will write it for free or you're going to pay some money to outsource it, which of course will ruin your goal of getting traffic to your site without spending a dime. It might be worth it however, because if the article isn't any good this technique is going to fail. So, make sure that this article that you write is as good as it can possibly be – as good as you would find on professional sites within your industry.

What this article will be about is a group of people who have expertise in the field that you are in, or even people in other fields. You don't necessarily have to stick within your own niche when it comes to this technique. You could write an article about the best bloggers to follow or the top entrepreneurs for the current year or the top experts in your own field. As previously mentioned, top 10 lists work exceptionally well for this, so make yours a top 10 list of whichever group of people you have chosen.

After you have written the article and published it, make sure that it was as good as it could possibly be, you can then contact the people who you wrote about and let them know that you have written an article about them and their expertise. Depending on their level of notoriety or your own level of expertise, they may or may not respond by linking to your article. Some of them will. Whoever does is going to give you a great deal of traffic to your site, which is the goal of this.

The great thing about this particular method is that you can use it so many different ways and you can use it over and over. So, you could write about the top 10 entrepreneurs and then you can follow it up with an article about bloggers or web designers or whoever it is that you think might be able to drive traffic to your site. If they have the ability to influence others and the traffic that they could drive to your site might convert then it's worth writing an article about them.

How to Know Which People to Choose for Your Article

Figuring out who to choose for your article isn't

all that difficult but it does take some research. What you want to do is find the sweet spot between the people who would definitely be willing to link to you if you wrote an article about them and the people who have the greatest amount of influence or followers. Obviously, if you choose someone who is massively influential like the late Steve Jobs, they aren't really going to care that you wrote an article about them and they certainly are going to link to you from their site. This level of influencer has articles written about them all the time. They are going to care about a blog post naming them in the top 10 of anything.

On the other hand, you don't want to choose people who have no influence either. For one thing, that would make for a terrible article if you are writing about people who had no expertise and no influence, and putting them in the top 10 article. These people would be perfectly willing to link to your article if you wrote about them but they can drive traffic to your site. So, you have to find the perfect combination of someone who is influential but smalltime enough to still be willing to link to your article if you write about them.

Sample Email to an Influencer That You Have

Written about

Name,

I have been following your career and I have considered you an expert in {NameofIndustry}, which is also an industry that I'm involved in. I recently wrote an article about the top 10 (insert article title) and you are one of those 10 experts that I named. I wanted to let you know, and say that I appreciate your contribution to the field. You can contact me if you have any questions. Here is a link to the article in question. (LINK TO ARTICLE HERE)

Sincerely,

Your Name

you@yourwebsite.com

In this chapter, were going to go over how viral reports can lead to huge traffic increases for your website. You can use this method to get traffic several different ways, and will discuss some of them here. You have to know how to write the report, and what to include in it, and then how to market effectively so that other people share for you. A viral report that is being passed around the Internet can generate a huge amount of traffic for you if you do it right. Here is what you need to know about the viral report method.

How to Create a Viral Report

So, the first thing that you're going to have to do is create the viral report. This means that you're going to have to choose a topic in your industry and then write about it but there are some very specific things that you need to include in this report in order to make it viable for this traffic technique. First of all, you need to make it something so revolutionary and so exciting the people are going to want to share it. This is an extremely tall order but unfortunately, you'll have to figure out yourself how to do it because any advice given here would only apply to a specific industry and not to creating a viral report in general.

However, the second thing that you need to be aware of is that the solutions that you list in this viral report need to either be solved by a particular website or by a product or service that is on that website. That's because you are going to list your own website as a solution for this report. Coming up with viral report material will take up the majority of the time you spend on this project because you need to make a good enough for people to share it; here are some examples of viral reports that might be solved by a particular website and could be shared.

10 Websites That Could Increase Your Traffic 500% in the Next 12 Months

12 Solutions to Organizing Your Life and Finally

Reaching Your Goals

Five Online Services That Could Double Your Income by the End of the Year

Do you get the idea? These are all reports that have websites is the solutions and that might be good enough to be shared by others. You have to make sure that the problem that is solved by the report is an experienced by only a tiny portion of the population – but as many people as possible. That doesn't necessarily mean that you have to appeal to every single person out there.

For example, with the popularity of singing reality shows you could easily write a report on improving your singing voice enough to pass in addition with American Idol or one of the other reality shows out there. This might not be shared with everyone, because not everyone is interested in singing or and auditioning for reality show, but there are enough people out there to drive traffic to your website if the report went viral.

Make Your Website One of the Options, Not the Only Option

One thing that you're going to want to keep in

mind is that you want the report to appear unbiased and as a public service to the people that are reading it. That means that you want to give them options – not just your own website is an option but also several others. 10 total websites is a good number and as previously mentioned, 10 seems to do really well for these type of reports or articles. When someone reads your report, you're going to want them to consider it legitimate enough to share with other people, particularly through social media or on their own website or blog. This means camouflaging your website among all the others so it doesn't appear as if your site is getting any special treatment but is included as a legitimate option or solution.

It is also worth noting that your website should actually solve the problem that the report is proposing to solve. If you list your website as a way to drive traffic, and people get there and realize that you have nothing to offer report, if they haven't shared it yet they're certainly not going to after that, and even if they have shared it they're going to stop sharing it further.

How to Get the Report out There

In order to distribute your report and give it its best chance of going viral, you want to get it in the hands of as many people within the industry as possible. You want to make it very clear to these people that the report is free of charge and they can pass it along to anyone they choose without any repercussions. Make sure you also put in the report itself the people can pass it along to their friends, colleagues or whoever.

When it comes to getting traffic to your website, there are lots of ways that you can go about it. In this book we have covered some of the ways that you can do it absolutely free-of-charge, including some revolutionary new methods that could potentially drive huge amount of traffic to your website.

But when you do have the budget for it, you should look into some of the paid ways that you can drive traffic to your site. However, just like with the free methods, you should look outside the box and not use traffic generation techniques that everyone seems to be selling these days. Instead, you should look at your own ideas and then use your budget to supplement them and make them even better.

A Summary of the Material in This Book

Make sure that your website is as professional-looking and clean as it can possibly be, with the right trust symbols, the right color scheme and a winning, up-to-date design.

Use viral blogging to get people to share your content driving traffic directly back to your website by using the most common types of shared content such as top 10 list, celebrity news and controversial topics.

Use YouTube to get people on that site to what your videos and then drive traffic from YouTube back to your own website.

Put a link to your website in your forum signature on every related forum that you visit, and then post whenever you can, making sure to reply to other people's posts, answering questions and giving advice.

Look for other sites that are selling related products and find the ones that will have a thank you page after the person buys the product that might trade links with you on that thank you page. You put their link on your thank you page and they put your link on theirs.

Use podcasting, with a professional sound, to build your expertise in the industry and drive traffic back to your website.

Find other websites that allow guest posting and then email them for a chance to post on their blog. You can build your expertise that way and include a link to your own website, and then their visitors will become your visitors.

Hold a free webinar on some type of specific topic within your industry and then invite every single person that you can, even letting people who are influential in the industry know that you're having a free webinar so they can tell all their followers as well.

Join social networking groups so that people will want to follow you on social media and then post expert content within these groups so that people will want to look you up and follow any links that you can post back to your own website.

Use the name dropping method to get people to link to your site simply because you have mentioned them in an article that you have written.

Finally, use the viral report method. Create a report that solves a problem within your industry and name your website as one of the solutions, and then distribute that report as widely as you can allowing people to share it freely.

IMPORTANT: To help you further take action, print out a copy of the *Checklist* and *Mindmap* I provided. You'll also find a Resource Cheat Sheet with valuable sites, posts and articles that I recommend you go through.

www.ingramcontent.com/pod-product-compliance
Lightning Source LLC
Chambersburg PA
CBHW061019050326
40689CB00012B/2683